Artificial Cherry

Artificial
CHERRY

Billeh Nickerson

ARSENAL PULP PRESS VANCOUVER

ARTIFICIAL CHERRY
Copyright © 2014 by Billeh Nickerson

All rights reserved. No part of this book may be reproduced in any part
by any means—graphic, electronic, or mechanical—without the prior
written permission of the publisher, except by a reviewer, who may use brief
excerpts in a review, or in the case of photocopying in Canada, a license
from Access Copyright.

ARSENAL PULP PRESS
Suite 202–211 East Georgia St.
Vancouver, BC V6A 1Z6
Canada
arsenalpulp.com

The publisher gratefully acknowledges the support of the Canada Council
for the Arts and the British Columbia Arts Council for its publishing
program, and the Government of Canada (through the Canada Book
Fund) and the Government of British Columbia (through the Book
Publishing Tax Credit Program) for its publishing activities.

Book design by Gerilee McBride
Editing by Susan Safyan

Printed and bound in Canada

Library and Archives Canada Cataloguing in Publication:

Nickerson, Billeh, 1972–, author
        Artificial cherry / Billeh Nickerson.

Poems.
Issued in print and electronic formats.
ISBN 978-1-55152-540-2 (pbk.).—ISBN 978-1-55152-541-9 (epub)

        I. Title.

PS8577.I32A77 2014   C811'.6   C2014-901433-3
                                             C2014-901434-1

For Sheri-D

Contents

Shelagh Rogers Called Me a Slut and Other True Stories

Crushes

Bŏd'ē

Highway Game: Anal RVs

The Anal Explorer, the Anal Safari, the Anal Siesta,
the Anal Ambassador, the Anal Diplomat, the Anal Dynasty,
the Anal Maverick, the Anal Outlaw, the Anal Renegade,
the Anal Retreat, the Anal Stampede, the Anal Jamboree,
the Anal Unity, the Anal Infinity, the Anal Tradition,
the Anal Landmark, the Anal Heartland, the Anal Harmony,
the Anal Chalet, the Anal Chateau, the Anal Winnebago.

The Anal Pinnacle, the Anal Prestige, the Anal Premier,
the Anal Shamrock, the Anal Leprechaun, the Anal Nugget,
the Anal Elegant Lady, the Anal Little Guy, the Anal Little Joe,
the Anal Palomino, the Anal Puma, the Anal Cougar,
the Anal Hurricane, the Anal Cyclone, the Anal Sandstorm,
the Anal Inferno, the Anal Voltage, the Anal Zinger,
the Anal Crescendo.

The Ghost of Blowjobs Past

Suppose you're invited to a Christmas party,
and when you arrive at the condo lobby
something feels familiar,
which is strange since it's not your kind
of building and you don't recall
ever coming there before.
Suppose on the flight up
it hits you that the building
occupies the space once home
to your favourite nightclub,
Luv-A-Fair or Love My Hair,
as you affectionately called it,
and even though the elevator plays Christmas carols,
your head starts to fill
with the thump thump thump
of the club along with visions
of your favourite bartenders,
the punk rock cocktail waitresses,
the woman with the long brown hair,
who you swear wore the same black dress

as she danced on the speakers
over a decade's worth of Tuesdays,
all this and more comes back to you
as you exit the elevator,
and just as you knock-knock-knock
on the door you're taken back to the moment
a beautiful stranger pushed you into the stalls
and gave you your first anonymous blowjob.
As the host opens the door
instead of saying hello you say,
Someone gave me a blowjob here
twenty years ago,
which makes him a little uncomfortable
and you a lot ashamed.
This isn't the first time
ghosts have haunted you
as most of Vancouver feels like a graveyard
of nightclubs past,
and even by just walking around
you're bound to realize

just how many of your pivotal moments

have been cemented over

like Jimmy Hoffa.

Maybe it's just ego

not being able to let go

of geography

or your need for connection,

a little bit of ownership

in a city you'll never own.

My Montreal Vagina

At times I've wondered
how it would be

to know its deep well
from within,

not just some visitor
fumbling around

as if searching for keys
in a pocket or purse,

but since it's unlikely
I'd ever have that opportunity

I never lamented the loss
of what could never have been

until I was surprised
by a doctor in Montreal

whose medical chart
perplexed him so deeply

he spent an entire minute
alternating between

looking at me and then
back down at his chart again

Do you have a vagina?
Do you own a vagina?

and part of me wondered
if only for a few moments

whether this was my chance
to say *Yes, I do*

to that chorus of well-meaning
friends who liked to joke

it didn't matter
I didn't have a vagina

because my asshole was my vagina
only in disguise.

So, you are a man then? With a penis?
You are a man without a vagina?

Yes, I'm a man, I said,
a man without a vagina,

though, for a few moments,
I fell in love with the possibility

of what a misplaced medical chart
could offer my anatomy,

my Montreal vagina appearing
as if by magic

then diving back in
to the well of itself.

Anthony's Glass Eye

I'd only heard of glass eyes
from the punk band
Sandy Duncan's Glass Eye—
Sandy Duncan, famous for flying
around stages in green leotards
thanks to a harness and wires,
famous for Peter Pan, Triscuit commercials,
and her glass eye, which made the flying
even more remarkable for some reason.

I'd only heard of glass eyes from that band
and her until I met Anthony
who'd surprise his roommates
by whipping out his penis,
pulling back the foreskin,
and inserting his glass eye
at the tip—a miniature Cyclops.

In my dreams, Anthony played marbles
with that eye as well, suckered all the kids
in the schoolyard every lunch hour,
wiped off his eye on his clean shirt
then popped it back in
just in time for class.

Perhaps it was Anthony who should have played
Peter Pan, perhaps Sandy Duncan
was mythological and could fly
without the harness and wires,
perhaps they shared the same designer
who'd hand blow little spheres
with love and care;
each one familiar, yet one of a kind.

Dorothy Stratten's Tent Trailer

When I overhear my parents talk
about the death of Dorothy Stratten,
the Playboy playmate first discovered
in a Vancouver Dairy Queen,
I somehow confuse her with the woman
who sold my family our tent trailer.
For show-and-tell that week, I announce:
The woman who sold my family our tent trailer
was murdered, and the teacher just nods her head
and moves on to the next child, a girl
who shows a doll she received for her birthday.
At the time, I'd only known of death
from young birds who fell from their nests,
a few flushed goldfish, and my mother's scissors
as she cut newspaper obituaries
she'd later place inside her Bible.

That a famous person—a famous person

who sold my family our prized tent trailer—

has died makes weekend getaways even more exotic:

Each time we camp that summer, I lie awake

listening to the crickets through the tarp walls,

thankful, yet still uncertain whether my happiness

somehow led to Dorothy's demise.

Five Things Men in Bed Have Told Me about Their Assholes

1.

I wasn't sure if you liked a waxed hole or not so I only did one side.

2.

All the men in my family are blessed with tight assholes.

3.

My hole's so deep you can fuck me all the way to China.

4.

My asshole can lip-synch Mariah Carey.

5.

In a previous life, my asshole must have been a heart.

Apartment Hunting in Toronto

No amount of panties or dirty sheets,
no amount of unflushed toilets
could have prepared me for the intimacy
of that used pregnancy test
beside the bananas
on the kitchen counter.

It didn't matter the tenant wasn't there
or the building manager
seemed not to notice
for that pregnancy test loomed
as large as the CN Tower,
shadowed everything in its wake.

Voting for Dr Hedy Fry

I'm voting for Dr Hedy Fry
because she's seen my vagina,
my friend tells me at a party
just before the federal election.
She's seen it many times.
And I trust her.

Mary's Breasts

—For Mary Belgue 1965–2005

During those last few months
people remarked on the difficulty
seeing her once voluptuous body
now bird-like and beyond skinny.

The breasts once celebrated
as the Best Tits in Town,
now flat and vulnerable,
a little girl's.

In gay clubs, drag queens
would fawn over her,
then squeal with delight
when told her breasts were real.

Men would often ogle,
as would women, and sometimes
babies in passing strollers
would reach up to her chest
in expectation.

Even now, Mary's breasts
rub up against me,
a busty guardian angel
who cushions my way.

Scrotal Eclipse of the Heart

When your boyfriend screams
from the bathroom
that his loose-hanging balls
dipped into the toilet water,
you don't have the heart to explain
it wasn't the water level
that betrayed him,
just gravity replaying
Sir Isaac Newton
and his apples.

Rebirth

The first time I shave my head
right down to the scalp,
I can't stop caressing
all that skin.

Everything feels new again,
especially the spider web
strung between two trees,
my bald head pushing through.

Life and Limb

One day we find ourselves perplexed
why thumbs are worth much more than fingers
after our teachers hand out insurance brochures
that list payouts for body parts.

Jason says it's because people love
video games and hitchhiking,
that they could be stranded
along roadsides without their thumbs.

Most of us have never considered
our bodies worthy of compensation,
our dirty fingernails and scratched-up knees
valued for nothing other than play.

Jonathan says it's just like the tooth fairy,
only there's no pillow and you get more
than a few coins or a crumpled-up dollar
to spend at the corner store.

On the news that night a reporter
talks about *the loss of life and limb*
and I wonder about the families,
which magical fairy will itemize their claims?

Pacific Northwest Elvis Festival

Pacific Northwest Elvis Festival

Colour of Cadillac parked outside festival reception: pink

Number of participating Elvis Tribute Artists: 21

Most imposing refreshment stand on shores of Okanagan Lake: giant peach-shaped building

Slush flavour options served from giant peach: blue, raspberry, and peach

Number of grilled peanut butter and banana sandwiches sold by day two of the festival by Sacha's Concession: 40

Most admirable quality of Elvis fans compared to other festival-goers, according to Sacha: Elvis fans clean up after themselves

Most overplayed Elvis song, according to Sacha: "Hound Dog"

Number of drunken Elvises reported to on-site security: 0

Most incomprehensible arrangement of items in merchandise booths: Julio Iglesias poster at centre of a profusion of Elvis magazines, posters, pop cans, and other paraphernalia

Number of days per year, according to Dorian, a local chain-mail artisan and musician, that residents have the Elvis Festival pushed on them, compared to tourists, who only have to put up with it for the duration of the festival: 365

Number of chain-mail bikini tops sold by Dorian to Elvis fans: 0

Number of times a dozen donuts were delivered to Dorian while he answered the above two questions: 3

Most common dance coupling during performances: grandmas with grandchildren

Best way to distinguish a professional Elvis tribute artist from an amateur: the professional knows better than to wear dark briefs under his white jumpsuit

Combined number of years of performance experience racked up by members of the Roustabouts, an Elvis tribute band: 120

Number of Priscilla Presley tribute artists: 0

Cost of a ticket to the Tribute Artist Competition finals at the Trade and Convention Centre: $45

Cost of a ticket to the Rotary Pancake Breakfast at the Gyro Park band shell: $4

Name of the Hillside Estate Winery limited edition Elvis Festival wine: Graceland Gamay

Day job of Jeff Bodner, Official Amateur-Elvis Spokesperson: RCMP officer

Sole Elvis tribute artist of Asian descent at the festival: Alfred Lau, "The Singing Dentist"

Elvis encomium that drew the most applause at the Friends of Elvis Question and Answer Panel, uttered by Joe Esposito, Elvis's former road manager: "Elvis loved all animals."

Possible reason, according to Joe Esposito, that Elvis found Vancouver's Empire Stadium so big: Canadian football fields are longer than American ones

Reason, according to Joe Esposito, that he once threw Elvis's shoes into a river from a moving car: they smelled awful

Reason, according to Joe Esposito, that Elvis once threw up on him: Elvis didn't realize the crème de menthe he had been drinking was alcoholic

Number of World Champion Elvis Tribute Artists on the Question and Answer Panel who wore eyeliner: 1

Number of audience members at the panel discussion who claimed to have listened to Elvis from the womb: 1

Most popular festival apparatus: lawn chair

Most complained-about festival behaviour: people standing up near the stage and blocking the view of those seated in lawn chairs

Best festival disclaimer statement, as written in the Official Program: "Judges for the 2003 Penticton Pacific Northwest Elvis Festival attended a judging seminar to add consistency and fairness in judging the tribute artists at all the festival venues."

First-prize winner at the Tribute Artist Competition: Gino Monopoli (Toronto)

Shelagh Rogers Called Me a Slut and Other True Stories

Shakespeare Never Did This, Victoria

The stage for the *Shakespeare Never Did This* reading series
shares a wall with a strip club, a wall just thick enough to
shield the reading series' audience from the strip club's noise,
but not thick enough to soundproof it for the poets on stage,
like me. Tonight, an American navy ship is in town. Even
though I can't see the strippers, I can visualize what sorts of
moves the women perform, based on the sailors' cheers (no
small feat for a gay man). As I hear my own voice read the
words from the pages I hold in my hands, I visualize horny
sailors and the lovely sirens who enrapture them behind the
wall. For a brief moment, I consider stuffing my ears with
cloth and candle wax, but that seems a tad extreme.

IV Lounge, Toronto

When I show up to read at the IV Lounge, the emcee
is visibly upset and already a few drinks in. With every
introduction he seems more emotional and his words more
slurred. During his short intro before my reading, my spidey
senses start to tingle. The host begins to weep onstage as
he explains that a former featured reader—a dearly beloved
poet—passed away just a few days ago. He weeps some more
and then is unable to talk before mustering the energy to
call out the dead poet's name as he stands tall with his beer
raised in the air like a Canadian Statue of Liberty. He then
announces a moment of silence and bows his head. After a
few seconds he looks up, as if nothing unusual has happened,
and screams, "Our next reader is Billeh Nickerson!"

Pride Coffee House, Victoria

I am supposed to read just after a lesbian bongo player who wears a white muscle shirt and seems to be in a trance as she hits her bongos and sways her body to the rhythm. She keeps chanting the phrase *feminine protectSHUN, feminine protectSHUN, feminine protectSHUN*, then stops and stares dramatically at the audience and whispers, *What are they protecting us from?* She repeats this over and over again. This is the same venue where I once saw a drunken man recite awful rhyming love poems before turning his back to the audience, dropping his pants, and spreading his ass cheeks. While I do not intend to moon the audience, I *am* nervous about how well my poems will go over with the feminine-protection crowd. It turns out to be a fun night and, thankfully, none of us needs protection.

The Western Front, Vancouver

The spoken-word artists all show up late and read for far longer than they should. It's thirty degrees inside, and the old converted hall doesn't have air conditioning. People fan themselves with their hands and pull their moist clothes away from their bodies, which is difficult, especially for the men. It's almost eleven p.m. by the time I get on stage, and I am beyond pissed off. In what I must admit is a dream come true, I walk on stage, thank the audience for sticking around, and then proceed to admonish the readers who didn't stick to their allotted times. Tonight, I tell the audience, was the last night my elderly grandmother with terminal cancer was able to see me perform, but when folks read too long, she had to leave. This is, of course, a big lie, but well worth the dishonesty.

Word on the Street, Vancouver

I'm reading as part of the Poetry in Transit program on
a BC Transit bus parked outside the Vancouver Public
Library. I stand in the open space near a side exit door while
my audience sits on bus seats and crane their necks to see
me. As I read, I think about how this is the widest room I've
ever read to. Instead of trying to project my voice outward
toward my audience, as I'm used to doing at coffee shops
and theatres, I spend a lot of my time moving my head back
and forth as I read to each distant end of the bus. I imagine
this is how it feels to be a tennis umpire. Just as I start to feel
comfortable, I hear a strange sound that is part sigh and part
guttural moan. A large man walks onto the bus and then
closer and closer to me until he is standing only inches from
my face. I'm not sure what to do, so I just keep reading, even
though the audience can now barely see me, and to some of
them, it must look like the two of us are waltzing. Once I
get to the end of my poem, the man grunts and leaves.

The Dufferin Pub, Vancouver

A half-naked man, who is obviously one of the strippers for *Skank: An Evening of Questionable Taste*, walks up to me and says, "Hello, my name is Peter. Would you like to see my Polish sausage?" in an accent that I am initially uncertain is real until later in the evening when I realize he actually is from Poland. After my co-host for the evening leaves the green room, Peter runs full-tilt and slams me into the wall before kissing my face and rubbing himself up against me. Moments later, my co-host opens the door. "Billeh Nickerson, you whore!" he screams. No matter how hard I try to explain the wall-slamming and the unexpected "Polish sausaging," I am unable to convince him of my innocence.

Ginger 62, Vancouver

Arsenal Pulp Press's thirtieth-anniversary reading at Ginger
62 is scheduled to take place just a day after two planes crash
into the World Trade Center in New York City. People have
been asking if Arsenal's event will even happen. Everyone
says it's the end of irony, and the world will never be the
same. Irony is my bread and butter, but I do decide it will
not be a good idea to read my poem "If You Fit All Your
Lovers in an Airplane What Kind Airplane Would It Be?"
I tell myself I'm not self-censoring; I'm just being sensitive.
It takes years before I feel comfortable reading that poem
again.

Hotel Arts, Calgary

I read to a group of strangers in a room at the Hotel Arts
as part of Room Service/Poetry Between the Sheets at the
Calgary International Spoken Word Festival. I feel just as
much a bellboy as a poet as I oscillate between reading my
poems and offering up pillows so the audience can get more
comfortable. Everyone is sitting or lounging on the room's
large bed. All my life, I've fantasized about having a group
of people in my hotel bed. This is not what my fantasy looks
like. After the reading, I go into the bathroom to take home
all the extra toiletries (once a thrifty poet, always a thrifty
poet), but one of my audience members has already beaten
me to the soap. This makes me feel a little sad; I thought
my poems would be treasure enough. I take a shower cap
though, a shower cap that I will use at home to cover bowls
of leftovers in the fridge.

The PNE, East Vancouver

I'm one of seven poets staging *Haiku Night in Canada* at
the Telus Main Stage at the Pacific National Exhibition,
where two teams of poets read haiku about hockey at each
other while another poet referees and keeps score. We've
performed this shtick many times, but this is the first time
we've done so outside a literary festival. It's strange to see
poets dressed up in hockey gear, complete with fake black
eyes and mouth guards, but not as strange as the parade of
exuberant young people who dance past the stage to a cheesy
song about cultural diversity. At first glance, I wonder if they
are sponsored by Up with People. Maybe they *are* Up with
People. Our audience consists of half-curious, exhausted
parents of rambunctious children sitting around the grassy
knoll in front of the stage. At the start of our reading, the
audience stands for the national anthem just like they would
at an NHL game, then we begin our poems. It all smells
like greasy midway offerings: hockey haiku deep-fried and
dipped into ketchup.

Random Acts of Poetry, Vancouver

It's the second time I participate in Random Acts of Poetry,
a nation-wide literacy event in which poets read poems and
give free copies of their books to strangers who seem to
believe the poets are trying to sell them something or lure
them into a cult. I fast learn that the easiest way to gauge
whether someone will be open to a stranger reading them
a poem is to look for people with funny socks. During
a press stop in front of Vancouver's City Hall, which is
admittedly not very random, I wait to read a poem to then-
Mayor Larry Campbell, the former real-life city coroner
who inspired the hit Canadian television series *Da Vinci's
Inquest.* A newspaper reporter known for his Grinch-like
attitude keeps asking me, "But isn't this just a big gimmick?"
I mention something about the need for a little spectacle
and literacy, and how could he, as a newspaper reporter, not
want more people reading and enjoying words, but he can't
seem to get over the idea that it's all just a gimmick. I'm
introduced to the mayor, who compliments me on my red
plaid pants, and I read a poem to him while photographers
take pictures and the grumpy reporter stands in the
background, off camera, frowning.

Berton House, Dawson City

I stand on the lawn behind Pierre Berton's childhood home in Dawson City, Yukon, where I'm the writer-in-residence for the summer. There's a big party going on, complete with a gazebo-like canopy tent and a bunch of curious residents and tourists who have come by for free food, the chance to tour the house, and, possibly, just maybe, attend an author's reading. I'm also less than a hundred metres from the Robert Service cabin, where Parks Canada tour guides recite his poems and answer the questions of tourists, who, for the most part, have thick American or German accents. I'm supposed to give my reading and then announce three winners of gold nuggets for a writing contest sponsored by the local tourism board, but I am preoccupied with the fact that the public gets to tour the house as part of the festivities. Even though I've only stayed there for a few weeks, it feels like I've just given notice, and my landlord already wants to show my place to prospective tenants. Perhaps my nerves stem from an incident a few weeks earlier, when a couple, who thought Berton House was a museum, walked in on me wearing only my ginch, and I had to ask them to leave—twice.

The Next Chapter, Toronto

I'm at the CBC Studios in Toronto being interviewed for
Shelagh Roger's radio program *The Next Chapter*. I read a
few poems about fast food and then, somehow, it sounds
as if Shelagh has just called me a slut on national radio.
Shelagh, I say, *My mom could be listening*. Shelagh gives a
call-out to my mom and, after the interview, one of her
assistants tells me she's never heard Shelagh say "slut" on the
radio before. Even my cousin Ruth, who's a CBC producer
in Winnipeg, comments on the interview. A couple of weeks
later, a stranger asks me at a party, "Hey, are you the poet
Shelagh Rogers called a slut? I liked your poems."

Crushes

Artificial Cherry

The conversation begins with how
she's a casting director for commercials.

All kinds of things, she tells me,
campaigns, merchandise, corporate stuff.

We're at a party by a kitchen counter
covered in bowls of chips and dip.

I mention I'm a writer and she smiles,
dips a chip and then another.

What's the strangest thing you've cast?
I ask, and she mentions needing

to find a three-hundred-pound woman
willing to jump naked on a trampoline,

dips a chip again, and then tells me
about a cancer-awareness project

in which the producer described
cancer patients as looking *too sick.*

We auditioned healthy actresses instead,
had them fill out white paper slips

with the price it would take
to shave their heads.

I'm not sure how the subject comes up,
but the casting director mentions artificial cherry

makes her skin break out in hives,
and how she avoids not just the obviously artificial

but everyday items
like ice creams and pies

whose manufacturers believe real cherries
aren't real enough for our taste buds.

I can't believe they do that, I tell her
as she dips another chip.

She thinks I'm referring to the artificial cherry,
when I'm still stuck on those women

holding paper slips
as if they were given a say.

Crushes

high school crushes
still pop-a-wheelie
inside your heart

your heart
still crushes
on pop-a-wheelies

pop-a-wheelie
hearts
crush

your heart
still pops-a-wheelie
on crushes

crushes
still in your heart
pop-a-wheelie

pop-a-wheelies
still crush
your heart

Men in Trench Coats

All I knew was men in trench coats
would find you in a park

and sometimes they would open
their trench coats and sometimes not,

but you were supposed to be afraid
of their trench coats

especially if you were a girl
and it was late at night.

I first learned about it
while on the monkey bars

during lunch or recess or maybe
it was after school,

it doesn't matter when, really,
only that the experienced girl, the one

who claimed to have already smoked
a few cigarettes and drank a whole beer

said it was the worst thing
that could ever happen,

that other people wouldn't want to
talk to you anymore,

not even your brothers or father,
not even your uncle the policeman

could help you or do anything,
not even your mom.

The Party (circa 1985)

—For Lorna Crozier

Suppose co-workers throw you a going-away party
and when you arrive you're drawn to one co-worker in particular,

let's call her Jean, and unlike most days when she shows up
in a conservative blouse and medium-length skirt,

her hair brushed but nothing fancy, her face makeup-free,
suppose when you see Jean at your going-away party

you're taken by her red jumpsuit with shoulder pads
and how she's curled her hair into ringlets

that frame her large eyeglasses and big dangly earrings.
Suppose when you see Jean, you run up and scream

how amazing she looks, how much you love her new hairdo,
and how you're so happy she's found this part of herself

you knew existed, but never thought you'd see.
Suppose you greet another co-worker and another

and when you look around the room, it's filled
with chunky earrings and jumpsuits and big hair

and suppose you begin to realize the party's theme
is to dress like you, but instead of getting the joke right away

you spend the first five minutes complimenting everyone
on how good they look, how marvellous, and never better.

Suppose you tell this story to a friend who loves you dearly
and when he decides to write something in your honour

he can't stop thinking about the party,
where even in going away

you find poetry
in the least expected places.

From Haiku Night in Canada

The hockey chicken:
puck, puck, puck, puck, puck, puck, puck
puck, puck, puck, puck, puck

Gordie fucking Howe
Mario fucking Lemieux
Wayne fucking Gretzky

Hockey postage stamps
lick your favourite player
Who could ask for more?

At the therapist's
the goalie describes his pain
a puck to the heart

How Will We Line Our Bird Cages?

How will we line our bird cages
when there aren't any newspapers?

How will we line our bird cages
when there aren't any birds?

Compulsion

You are a small child
who finds a fish.

It's a dead fish
and you have a stick.

On another day it could be
Mexican jumping beans,

Mexican jumping beans
and a hammer,

but, today, it's that fish,
that dead fish,

a stick in your hand,
sand beneath your feet.

Petrified

—For Bernhard Friz

We were having drinks in his hotel room,
a rather ordinary occurrence given our long friendship
and penchant for meeting in random cities,

but this room offered an amazing view
of the floating gas station in Burrard Inlet
and the lights strung along the Second Narrows

as if there were a route
to heaven or at least some place fabulous
just a short drive away.

He remarked that there was a time
when even a crappy hotel room
presented an opportunity

to hook up with strangers,
and how peculiar it was that now,
when he finally had rooms with views

worthy of sharing,
the dread of putting in the effort
outweighed his desire to share.

In movies, loneliness is often depicted
as a rundown room
littered with empties

when really the loneliest moments
are those when we can't share
something spectacular.

Of all the things we talked about that night,
I remember most his excitement
about a recent museum visit

when the curator invited guests
to decipher between
petrified wood and bone

by placing fragments on their tongues
as even after 100,000 years
capillaries will still tug at your flesh.

It's pretty sad, he told me,
when an old bone's more romantic
than most of the guys I've dated.

Now I can't stop thinking
about the resiliency
of those capillaries,

the unviewed rooms
within ourselves
aching to be seen.

The Armadillo

Who could blame her
for bringing a dead mouse
to show and tell
when only a week earlier
some kid brought
a stuffed armadillo?

Who could blame her
for building it a house
out of a shoe box,
making furniture
from toilet paper rolls
and buttons and bottle caps?

Who could blame her
for not understanding
the minutiae of taxidermy
when she wanted only to share
her love, now so public
and misunderstood?

Nadia Comăneci

Just before the game, I took the Metro out to Village
des Valeurs (Value Village) to buy secondhand Montreal
Expos baseball caps for ninety-nine cents so my friends
and I would fit in with the other Expos fans, and then
at the stadium we discovered that the team changed its
uniform years ago. We wore the caps anyway because we
all had hat hair and that seemed worse. While waiting for
another group of friends, we stood beneath a photograph
of Nadia Comăneci, the Romanian gymnast and queen of
the 1976 Montreal Olympics, and I tried to explain the
whole Nadia phenomenon: the perfect tens, her little hair
ribbons, all those gold medals. No one remembered her and
that saddened me. Inside the stadium, I noticed that the
Goodyear blimp had turned into the Fuji Blimp. This was
the first major league game for the Expo pitcher, who hit a
two-bagger at his first at-bat, and when the board lit up with
his batting average, which at that moment was a perfect
1,000, I thought of Nadia's perfect tens again.

The Saint Baby Jesus Credit Union

In a story in the *Montreal Gazette*, the government agency that okays the names of newborn babies in Quebec rules that a couple from Montreal may not name their child "Ivory." An agency spokesperson claims that when the child grows older, classmates will tease her for being named after a bar of soap. In appealing the decision, the mother says that her child's name came to her in a dream, not from a bar of soap. The article mentions another couple first denied then given permission to name their child C'est-un-Ange (It's An Angel). I am reminded of these two babies when I pass La Caisse Populaire Saint-Enfant-Jésus—The Saint Baby Jesus Credit Union. What would have happened to the world if Mary had decided to name Jesus Ivory or C'est-un-Ange? Would God have stopped her or just let things take their course?

Colonel Sanders

The Dairy Queen on avenue du Parc reminds me of a truck
stop without the trucks and the greasy food, and a beachside
fish 'n' chips joint without the beach and the fish 'n' chips:
it's tiny and it only serves ice cream. My friend explains that
Dairy Queens in Quebec aren't like the Braziers in British
Columbia, and that they close for half the year when it's
twenty below. On the walk back home I notice that the
sign in front of Kentucky Fried Chicken reads "PFK." My
friend tells me that Quebecers still call Dairy Queen "Dairy
Queen," but they call Kentucky Fried Chicken "Poulet Frit
Kentucky" or "PFK" for short. When I ask her how to say
Colonel Sanders in French, she assures me it's still Colonel
Sanders.

Elvis and Jacques

At the laundromat on rue Saint-Viateur the proprietor
looks like Elvis or at least someone who would have looked
like Elvis if Elvis hadn't OD'ed on deep-fried peanut butter
and banana sandwiches. He turns to me and asks, "*Chaud
ou froid?*" I tell him, "One hot, two cold, and soap," and he
passes me a small yogurt container filled with detergent
and two sheets of fabric softener. I put the fabric softener
into my bag and later mistake it for Kleenex on the bus
to Ottawa when I blow my nose and everything starts
to smell like fresh pine. An Elvis collage and a display of
newspaper clippings about Jacques Villeneuve cover the
walls in one corner of the laundromat. The other walls are
crammed with community bulletin boards containing ads
for bilingual psychics, travel posters advertising an unnamed
tropical destination, and notices in three languages warning
customers not to overload the machines. My clothes spin
around the washers, and I wonder about the punishments
for overloading: my mother would make the culprits eat
laundry soap, and my father would send them into the
backyard to pile wood. By the time my wash cycle finishes, I
feel as if my life has somehow been saved.

The Proposal

—For Ivan E. Coyote

The woman on the plane tells me
her husband proposed while they were on a rowboat,

which strikes me as charming
until she mentions they were floating

on Loch Ness looking for the monster
while on an amateur research expedition.

She tells me the location wouldn't have been
her first choice for such an occasion

though her husband did manage
to keep the boat afloat while he scrambled

onto one knee and presented her
with the most beautiful ring ever.

He thought he was being romantic,
she says with a twinkle in her eyes

though it kinda creeped her out
committing to him at that moment,

given all the rumours and uncertainty
hidden beneath those waters.

She says she would have preferred
Disneyland or even a simple picnic

with the birds singing in the background
and the sun warming their skin,

so I offer up that Loch Ness
is a wonderful place for a proposal,

that maybe the monster was watching,
maybe he blessed her marriage somehow

with some ancient monster ritual
that only monsters know about,

but it seems to unsettle her
for she looks at me like I'm crazy,

a crazy person she must now sit beside
for the duration of our long flight together.

No, the monster never blessed us,
why would you say that?

Red Mailboxes

For months you avoid busy streets
and their red mailboxes,

which look like your ex
in his red ski jacket.

The red fire hydrant, the stop sign,
neither of these cause concern,

only that right size of red
in the distance

as if your ex realized
the futility of sending letters

and became the mailbox
instead.

Dogs and Dancing Shoes

Hobbled by micro strokes, my grandma forgets
each of the grandchildren
from youngest to eldest
then her youngest daughter
then the other siblings
until she starts to believe my father
is her husband.

When can we go dancing again?
Why won't you take me dancing?
she'll ask with a pouty look on her face
even though she hasn't danced in decades
and her body long ago lost the ability
to manoeuvre dance floors.

I feel for my father, never one to share
overt emotions with his own children.
I'll only hear of his patience
from my mother, who's once again thrust
into her role as familial liaison.

When can we go dancing again?
Why won't you take me dancing?

This reminds me of my mother's father,
who, just days before his death,
wakes up with the biggest smile on his face,
tells my mother he just dreamed
he was running with every dog he'd ever owned.
I imagine him running like that sometimes,
just as I imagine my father's mother
in her favourite dancing shoes, a swing band
serenading her with pomp and swoon.

Acknowledgments

Thank you to the editors of the following publications for including my poems:

Contemporary Verse 2 (CV2): "The Party (circa 1985)"

EVENT: "Shelagh Rogers Called Me a Slut and Other True Stories" was commissioned as part of their "Notes on Writing" annual issue.

"The Ghost of Blowjobs Past" appeared in Cabico, Regie and Brittany Forte, eds. *Flicker and Spark: A Contemporary Queer Anthology of Spoken Word and Poetry*. Northfield, MN: Lowbrow Press, 2013.

Geist: "Dorothy Stratten's Tent Trailer"; "The Penticton Pacific Northwest Elvis Festival"; and "The Saint Baby Jesus Credit Union"

Poetry Is Dead: "Anthony's Glass Eye" and "Five Things Men in Bed Have Told Me About Their Assholes"

PRISM international: "My Montreal Vagina"; "Petrified"; and "Red Mailboxes"

subTerrain: "The Ghost of Blowjobs Past" appeared in their Vancouver 125 issue and was read at the Vancouver 125 Poetry Conference

Thank you to the owners and staff at Turk's Coffee Bar on Commercial Drive for putting up with the strange guy whispering and mouthing his poems to himself in the corner.

Thanks to all the fine folks at Arsenal Pulp Press.

Special thanks to Elizabeth Bachinsky, Ivan E. Coyote, Michael V. Smith, Sheri-D Wilson, and Daniel Zomparelli for reading and listening to earlier versions of this manuscript, and all my friends who gave—usually—late-night feedback.

PHOTO: Michelle Brayton

Born in Halifax and raised in Langley, BC, BILLEH NICKERSON is the author of the poetry collections *The Asthmatic Glassblower*, *McPoems*, and *Impact: The Titanic Poems* as well as the humour collection *Let Me Kiss It Better*. He is also co-editor of *Seminal: The Anthology of Canada's Gay Male Poets*, and past writer-in-residence at both Queen's University in Kingston, Ontario and Berton House in Dawson City, Yukon. He is also a silver medalist at the Canadian Gay Curling Championships, and Chair of the Creative Writing department at Kwantlen Polytechnic University in Vancouver.